Golf: a beginner's guide

Carroll Diaz

Stanford University

National Press Books

Library of Congress Catalog Card Number: 73-93342

International Standard Book Numbers: 0-87484-216-6 (paper)
0-87484-217-4 (cloth)

Manufactured in the United States of America

National Press Books, 285 Hamilton Avenue, Palo Alto, California 94301

Sponsoring editor: Richard W. Bare
Editor: London Green
Designer: Nancy Sears
Photographer: Dick Keeble
Models: Shelly Hamlin and Mark McBride
Production: Michelle Hogan

Contents

Foreword

Good golfing cannot be learned entirely on one's own. A qualified instructor is *essential* to eliminate bad habits, poor playing techniques, and the frustration that causes so many inadequate golfers to give up what can be a wonderfully satisfying recreational activity. So this is not a "do-it-yourself" book. It is meant to serve as a detailed aid to the qualified instructor and as a guide to his students.

Qualified instruction is the primary concern for the beginning golfer. Friends, relatives, and other golfers may offer interesting tips, but they are not professionals and will probably do more harm than good. A professional instructor can offer not only the proper techniques for play but also the continuity and progression of techniques that are essential for real improvement.

This book is the result of the author's twenty years of teaching experience and twenty-eight years of playing the game. It is the result of continued experience, observation, and conversation with beginning, advanced, and professional golfers. Included are a glossary and a list of outstanding books that will supplement the player's knowledge and understanding of the game.

It is axiomatic that no one learns the game through reading, however. This manual gives a basis of technique on which to build a game, provides concepts, and explains procedures. If these rules and techniques, learned in cooperation with a qualified teacher, are followed, the beginning golfer should be able to play his first game with considerable confidence and enjoyment.

Lessons are generally available for people of all ages in a variety of circumstances. Ideally a person should begin taking lessons at the age of about ten. Maturity, ability, and desire to play are, of course, of great importance. Playing *too* soon may frustrate the child to the point where he learns to hate the game. Unfortunately, relatively few junior high schools offer golf classes. However, there are broad opportunities to learn the game under competent supervision in high schools, colleges, and public and private clubs. Many cities, for example, have a recreational program for golf beginners. *Golf: A Beginner's Guide* has been designed as a clear and complete guide for instructors and students of this overwhelmingly popular sport.

Introduction

"What possible satisfaction can you get from walking all afternoon just to hit a little white ball?"

Confirmed non-golfers always ask that question, and even lifetime enthusiasts cannot always explain the fascination and challenge of the game: the deep satisfaction in that peculiar combination of muscular freedom and control that sends the little white ball off on accurate flight.

According to historians, the Dutch were the first to play golf, although the Scots certainly made the game famous. Perhaps they were a bit too enthusiastic: in 1457 the Scottish Parliament, disturbed that football and golf had lured young Scotsmen from the more soldierly practice of archery, adopted an ordinance that "futeball and golf be utterly cryit down and nocht usit." However, in the seventeenth century James I and Charles I of England became golf enthusiasts, and the sport became known as "the royal and ancient game of golf."

In those days golf balls were made of leather and stuffed with feathers, but in about 1850 gutta-percha balls replaced the leather ones. In 1860 formal competition began in England with the estabment of an annual British Open tournament. In the United States there are indications that golf was played even in colonial times, but detailed records do not come until 1888, when in Yonkers, New York, a man named John Reid and his friends laid out a six-hole course on the Reid estate and formed the St. Andrew's Golf Club. For many years the game was regarded by the American public as an essentially aristocratic pastime. In 1913, however, that attitude changed dramatically when Francis Quimet, a twenty-year-old former caddy, came from Boston to Brookline, Massachusetts for the first United States Open championship to defeat two great British professionals, Harry Vardon and Ted Ray. Such a great victory generated enthusiasm throughout the country. In 1930 Bobby Jones of Atlanta astonished the country—and the world—by winning four championships: the U.S. Open, the U.S. Amateur, the British Open, and the British Amateur. Today the game of hitting the little white ball is truly a national pastime.

The Grip *

In golf, the swing, and not the grip, is often regarded as of greatest importance. However, the *final control* of the stroke lies in the grip—the connecting link between the golfer's body and the clubhead. The power and control of the body are transmitted through the hands; if the hands function with controlled freedom throughout the swing, the club will hit the ball squarely and solidly.

Power.   The power of the golf swing originates in the golfer's body. This power is then transferred to the arms, and through the hands to the clubhead. When the grip is correct, the power multiplies significantly at each point of transfer, much as in the children's game of Snap-the-Whip, in which the end of the chain travels many times faster than the hand which originated the action.

To put it simply, *if the grip does not work, nothing else will!*

Styles of Grip.   There are three primary styles of gripping the club: the overlapping, the unlap, and the interlocking. The overlapping style is preferable because it provides the best coordination be-

*All hand references in this manual are intended for the right-handed golfer. The left-handed golfer should follow the same instructions, but should reverse the direction and movements.

tween the hands, allowing them to operate smoothly and efficiently.

First, place your left arm along the left side of the body, hanging straight down so that the thumb is aligned with the side seam of your clothes. Then place your club in the left hand between the thumb and forefinger so that the shaft extends one-fourth of an inch above the heel of the thumb. The fingers wrap around the club. You then bring the club forward in front of the body so that the V formed by the thumb and forefinger points toward the right shoulder.

Then move the right hand down the shaft to overlap with the left hand. The little finger of the right hand is placed over the knuckle of the index finger of the left hand. The ring, middle, and index fingers and the fleshy part of the thumb should contact the club. (See figures 1 and 2.) Looking down the shaft, you should see the bottom knuckles of the forefinger, middle finger, and ring finger. The right thumb and forefinger should form a "hook" when the right hand is closed to contribute a "feel" to the swing. You should never loosen the left-hand grip because it acts as a guide throughout the entire swing. The overall feel must be "fingers against palms."

The palms of the hands should face each other, with the shaft lying diagonally across the left hand. The back of the left hand should face toward the target. At this point, the V formed by the thumb and forefinger of the left hand should point toward the player's right shoulder. The thumb of the left hand should rest slightly on the right side of the shaft. By placing the thumb slightly above the knuckle of the index finger, the "short thumb" results—an element that is essential to a good grip.

To place the hands in the prescribed position is comparatively easy. To maintain the grip, however, is difficult, because the grip is unnatural. There is no other activity or "muscle memory" to which you can refer. The correct grip can come to seem natural only with the discipline of repeated practice.

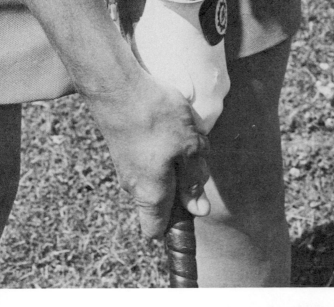

1
Hand position: palms
face each other and back
of hand faces toward
target

2
Hand position: note
fingers of right hand

Two other grips are sometimes used: the unlap and the interlocking. The "unlap grip" uses the same hand placement as the overlapping, except that the little finger of the right hand is placed on the club rather than over the index finger of the left hand. This grip is primarily for the use of golfers with short fingers.

Although the interlocking grip is sometimes taught, it is not recommended. In this grip the hands are placed on the club exactly as in the overlapping grip, with the following exception: the left index finger is removed from contact with the club and placed between the little finger and ring finger of the right hand. However, the author considers the overlapping grip superior to the interlocking grip because it provides better coordination between the hands, allowing them to operate with maximum smoothness and efficiency.

Whichever grip is used, it should be consistently and constantly practiced, and the hands, wrists, and fingers should be strengthened by regular exercise. Often the weakest element in a golfer's performance—particularly among women—is the use of the hands. For exercise many golfers squeeze a rubber ball, a stick, or a pencil in order to increase the strength of their hands and wrists, much as boxers do.

Aims.   You must work not only for strength but also for accuracy in directing your club. The club should not be held in a "death grip." The hands should be held as closely together as possible, to act in unison in transferring power and providing control. On the other hand, the grip should not be too loose, since you must maintain throughout the swing a fixed relationship between your hands and the face of your club. A loose grip will allow the club to turn and cause you to loose control.

The use of a glove is optional. A beginner should use it only if it affords better control and he feels more comfortable wearing it.

In closing, it should be noted that a proper grip will keep your arms in the correct position also. The proper use of the arms is discussed in the section on the swing. Here it is enough to say that when the club is gripped correctly your arms will form a V and will remain in proper relationship throughout the swing. A correct grip, therefore, permits the hands, wrists, and arms to work as a unit rather than against each other.

Stance and Address

In golf, as in many other sports, bodily balance plays a major role in the achievement of success. Such balance is an essential element of the golfer's *stance*, which is actually the initial phase of the golfer's stroke. As such, the proper stance should be assumed with consistent care. Correct stance is essential, for example, to both comfort and rhythm in playing. Incorrect stance can result in improper pivoting and a poorly hit shot.

Legs. First assume a comfortable stride position that will afford good balance. As a guide, visualize a railroad track. (See figure 3.) Place the right foot at right angles to the "inside" track, with the toes touching the track. Place the left foot at a forty-five-degree angle against the same track. The "outside" track is the line along which the ball will travel to the target. This stance prevents you from turning your hips too far on the backswing and yet allows the hips and knees to turn fully toward the target on the downswing and follow-through.

In assuming this stance, you should normally place your feet as far apart as the distance between your shoulders. Your weight should be distributed equally between the feet and supported equally by the heels and balls of each foot. The weight on the feet

3   "Railroad track"

should never be forward, nor should it ever rest on the clubhead at the point of contact with the ball. In gauging the proper distance to stand from the ball, consider yourself a tripod, with the feet and clubhead as three points of contact with the ground. (See figure 4.)

Your knees should be slightly bent and moved toward one another, so that there is a feeling of being slightly knock-kneed. (See figures 5 and 6.) The knees should be flexed, but not too much so. You should be comfortable rather than rigid, but also ready for action. Your weight should be evenly distributed on the inner sides of both feet.

By flexing the knees and assuming a somewhat relaxed position, you eliminate the danger of assuming too wide a stance and "digging in," which can prevent proper motion of the feet and shifting of weight during the swing. By distributing your weight evenly on the inner sides of the feet, you can maintain a sufficiently solid stance for proper hitting.

Posture.   Lastly, your body should be inclined slightly forward, to allow the arms to swing freely back and forth without touching the body. The distance between the shaft end of the club and the body should equal the length of the hand. Avoid *reaching* for the ball: this will pull the arms away from the body and flatten the swing. Because of the hand position on the club, the right shoulder will be somewhat lower than the left and the body will be slightly tilted.

Although the body is inclined forward, your back should not be bent or curved. The chin should be raised slightly and, in effect, in line with the ball. Your eyes should concentrate on the back of the ball, not the top. As indicated in the analogy of the tripod above, the back of the ball should be placed centrally in relation to your stance (except for wood shots, in which the ball is in line with the left heel). It should be noted that for people wearing bifocals, lenses are available to provide a correct perspective.

4
Relationship
between feet and
clubhead

5   Knee position

6   Knee position, side view

Relaxation. When the proper position has been assumed, check to see that you have maintained some degree of relaxation. When you are ready to swing with the proper grip, stance, and posture, you should *lessen* your tension and get set to drive the ball down that railroad track.

You are now addressing the ball and are ready to swing.

The Swing

A correct swing is basic to success in the game of golf. Its importance as a separate element is indicated in the following story. During World War II a woman confined in a German concentration camp found an old golf club. She had never played, but a fellow inmate and former golfer taught her the proper method of swing. They had no ball: just the club. Over the years, their sole diversion was practicing the fundamentals of the swing, which they performed an incalculable number of times. After the war, the woman emigrated to America. Here she played her first full round with an unfamiliar object called a golf ball on an unfamiliar stretch of grass called a golf course. Although her exact score was not recorded, it is said to have been in the low eighties: the envy of the nineteenth-hole crowd.

As noted in the previous chapter, a correct swing begins with a comfortable and balanced stance and address, from which the golfer can project the ball along the "railroad track" mentioned. Unnecessary tension or muscle strain will only defeat the golfer, who in addition must have a very clear conception of the manner and direction in which he intends to hit the ball.

Rhythm.   In developing a proper swing, you must come to sense the importance of correct rhythm and timing, without which a smooth swing is impossible. A smooth swing results from a succession of positions which are comfortable and unhampered by excess muscular tension. These positions must be practiced to the point at which they become natural and are assumed unconsciously by means of "muscle memory."

Preliminary Exercises.   Before practicing with a club, you will find it valuable to practise two empty-handed swing exercises. The first exercise involves swinging the arms together. After assuming the stance described above, join your palms, forming a V with your arms. You then swing your arms gently and rhythmically forward and backward (in relation to the "ball"). The motion should resemble that of a pendulum or an elephant's trunk. The exercise should be repeated for at least five minutes before using a club.

The second exercise involves swinging the arms while steadying your head. You swing while leaning your forehead forward (in the proper position) against a wall or the extended hand of a partner. This will give you the sensation of keeping your head steady, a concept you should keep in mind later when playing or practicing.

Even in these preliminary exercises, the relative tension and position of the arms should be considered. The left arm should be extended and firm, since it provides power for the swing. The right arm should be "soft" and slightly flexed, to prevent it from overpowering the left arm.

During this exercise, and in playing, you will pivot: your ankles will tend to roll toward the ground as your hips and shoulders rotate and your weight shifts to your right foot during the backswing. (See figure 7.) As this happens, your left knee should break in towards the right knee. In turn, your hips will make a one-quarter turn in the direction of the backswing, and your shoulders will turn slightly more than that. This pivot should occur *naturally* in the

7   Shift of weight during backswing

8   Flexing the wrists

course of the swing: you should make no conscious attempt to twist your waist or to drop your left shoulder. In summary, the pivot results from swinging the club in a wide arc. The left foot, knee, hip, and shoulder turn toward the right. The head should remain steady, as in the second preliminary exercise.

Swinging.   You are now ready to practice the full swing technique. During instruction and practice it is best to use a No. 5 iron, which is of medium length and provides a moderate loft. In preparing for the swing, you should assume the correct stance and hold the club directly in front of you, with the arms extended in a V position. You then should practice flexing and firming your wrists so that the club is perpendicular to the ground. (See figure 8.) The flexing of the wrists will demonstrate the proper wrist action during a shot: a wrist action which will keep the club "in the groove," supply the requisite power, and afford the proper "feel." You should then turn your back to the target and repeat the same exercise. (See figure 9.)

Following this exercise, practice flexing your wrists so that you push the clubhead over your shoulder to a point midway between the outer point of the shoulder and the base of the neck and then return to the original position. (See figure 10.) The path of the club should be in line with the target and parallel to our imagined railroad track.

Analysis.   All the elements of this swinging exercise must be analyzed in detail. First, the clubhead follows the "track" until it is just behind the right hip. Second, your shoulders and back naturally turn away from the target and then towards it again as the club comes down. Third, throughout the swing the arms should maintain a V. (See figure 11.) Fourth, if the hip action is correct, the weight will shift to the left leg almost automatically. Fifth, the head remains in its original position throughout the swing. Sixth, the proper grip must be maintained throughout the exercise. When you are at the

9   Back to target

10 Position of clubhead over shoulder

11   Maintaining the V

top of your swing, you must be certain that the thumbs are *under* the club, and *parallel* to the "rail," and pointing *towards* the target. Seventh, the left hand must guide the swing and the right hand must not overpower it. As the hands move up and out, the left arm must remain in a straight extended position, while the right arm bends. At the top of the swing you should have the feeling of holding a tray over your right shoulder in such a way that nothing will fall from it. (See figures 12 and 13.) At this point, you will have bent at the waist slightly toward the left and your head will naturally have dropped slightly toward the left. Eighth, during the forward swing, when the club arrives in the hitting area, you should not allow your left hand to turn or roll. (See figures 14 and 15.) The knees should face in the direction of the target.

This swinging exercise should be repeated until you achieve a comfortable feeling throughout your body. In practice you should *not* concentrate on any one element to the detriment of others. Stance, address, and grip are integral parts of a successful swing and must be practiced together.

After having mastered this exercise, you must practice reaching the finishing position (after having "hit the ball"). To do this you must repeat the above exercise, raising the clubhead over your *left* shoulder. In the reverse position, of course, the *right* arm is straight and the *left* bent.

The entire swing should now be practiced. Even though you are not yet working with a ball, keep in mind that your eventual goal will be not to chop at the ball but to achieve a smooth, uniform acceleration of the clubhead *through* the ball, so to speak. This acceleration requires a clubhead movement of nearly 360 degrees and a shoulder rotation of about 180 degrees. A second consideration is the height of the club from the ground at the point of contact with the ball. You should swing your club as though clipping the grass at ground level. Avoid digging holes in the grass.

In practicing the entire swing, a lime line can be used at first. It

12 "Holding the tray"

13   "Holding the tray," front view

14
Position before
impact

15
Position after
impact

should follow the line of the club from prior to hitting the ball through the beginning of the follow-through. The same effect can be achieved by placing two clubs on the grass about six inches apart. These devices are helpful to the beginning golfer but should not be used as a crutch.

When the "feel" of a good swing has been achieved, it must be practiced repeatedly. When you can swing consistently and confidently through the grass at the same point, you are ready to hit the ball.

Hitting the Ball

When you have learned the fundamentals of the swing, you will probably want to head for the nearest golf course to begin a round of play. However, your next stop should be not on a golf course but on a practice range, where you can continue to work on your stance and swing as you learn the art of meeting the ball properly with your club. Speeding up this vital learning process will more often than not result in retrogression and failure. Even the top professionals practice both before and after their most important tournaments.

Practice Range Rules. Two general rules should be followed on the practice range. During the first two weeks of practice, the sessions should last only half an hour. With longer sessions, your hands will become irritated and you will become tired and careless, making the same mistakes repeatedly. When both your hands AND you have become toughened, you can practice for longer periods of time. You should also take considerable time during these practice sessions to review what you have already learned. Check your grip constantly and carefully, since the position will not seem natural until after months of actual play. The "elephant trunk" swing exercise should also be performed repeatedly.

16
Lining up the
ball with the
target

In these practice sessions, follow a fixed procedure and progression of exercises.

After working on your stance, grip, and swing, line up the ball with the target (see figure 16) and assume the correct stance and grip. Check all the points covered in the chapters on those subjects. As you assume your stance, waggle your club (move it slightly back and forth) and shift your weight to attain proper balance. (See figure 17.) These movements, it should be remembered, are made only to attain proper balance and should not be accentuated or continued for an unusual length of time.

Analysis.   You are now ready to swing through. As you do this, be aware of a number of new points to check.

As a beginning golfer you must guard against an incomplete swing. When you first swing through, there is a great tendency to pull back too soon. In order to check on this, *hold* your finished position for a few seconds, mentally examining it. (See figure 18.)

Check your grip repeatedly. The principle clue that your grip is incorrect is the development of blisters on your hands. Blisters result from friction, a sure sign that the club is slipping and that the grip is incorrect. If blisters on the palms continue, consult the instructor. Blisters on the thumbs indicate a particularly incorrect grip. Such blisters are usually the result of pressing down on the club with the thumbs rather than with the fingers.

Missing the Ball.   You must realize that you will miss the ball occasionally—even frequently. When this happens step back from the ball and work on the "grass clipping" exercise mentioned earlier. At this early point, do not worry about the direction of the ball; it is important only that it takes flight. You can work on directional errors later.

Exercise.   After such preliminary work, you are ready to try an

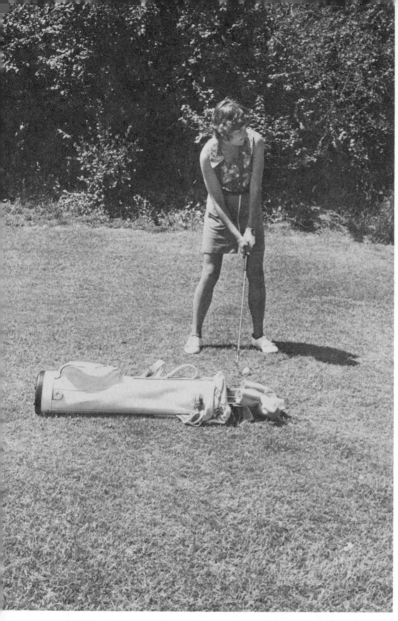

17 Attaining proper balance

18
Finished position

exercise called the "human robot," especially useful for the development of rhythm, balance, style, and directional accuracy. It is best practiced with a partner, for reasons explained below.

First, a series of balls is lined up, spaced at least the length of a clubhead apart. (See figures 19, 20, and 21.) You should use a 7 iron because of its length and loft. You then grasp the club halfway down the grip, take a stance at the end of—and perpendicular to—the line of balls, and briefly practice (without hitting the ball) at half-swing to develop a rhythm.

You then take a normal stance before the first ball and swing through. During the back swing, you step forward slightly with the right foot, and on the downswing step forward with the left foot. This action of stepping and hitting is repeated down the line of balls.

For efficiency and faster progress, work at first with a partner, who stands at the end of the line of golf balls and determines whether each ball is getting proper loft. So that you will get the "feel" of a good shot and will not be tempted to lift your head, the partner should call "good" on the appropriate shots. It is very important NOT to stop for corrections: to continue walking and hitting. The exercise should be repeated a number of times. At this point, if more than half the shots are good, the record is above average.

After repeated work with a partner, you can practice the exercise alone, using a half-swing, holding each finish, and determining yourself if each shot is good.

Direction.   The next step is to aim for direction. A flag or visible marker should be placed from thirty-five to forty yards from the point at which the ball is to be hit. Here the most important element is concentration. Before hitting the ball, draw an imaginary line between the ball and the target. You are not concerned with distance but with direction. If when you hit the ball it does not drop within ten yards on either side of the target line, go over your

19
Human robot (1)

20
Human robot (2)

21
Human robot (3)

checklist again. The list should now include stance, clubface position, grip, and swing. If these elements are correct, the ball will travel straight.

Distance.   After practicing hitting for direction, begin to work on hitting for distance. Using the same exercise as for direction hitting, begin with short shots, working up to longer ones as you strengthen your swing.

As you develop your ability and confidence in shooting for direction and distance, you should, if possible, play to a green. This is valuable in that it introduces you to actual playing conditions. If a green is not available, a flag should be placed at varying distances so that you can become accustomed to hitting from different angles and distances.

You are now ready to work on a putting green, but first become acquainted with the various kinds of clubs and other golf equipment available.

Clubs

Eventually you should practice with all of the basic clubs to develop confidence and authority in using them. The same basic swing is used with all clubs, except for the putter. Ball placement is as described, except for the woods, when the ball is placed in line with the left heel.

Woods. The woods are used for distance. The No. 1 wood has a straight clubface and is therefore used for the longest and least lofted shots: most commonly tee shots and low shots on the fairway.

The No. 2 wood is also known as the brassie. It is a more efficient club than the No. 1 because it has a higher loft. It is a fairway wood that is used for a "good lie" and should be used when the ball is on a cushion of grass similar to a tee. Practically speaking, however, it is seldom used on most golf courses because of their poor condition.

The No. 3 wood, or "spoon," is used on the fairway for a normal lie, and has a little more loft than a No. 2.

The No. 4 wood is used if there is a bad lie on the fairway, if there is little turf, if the ball is in a divot with little grass underneath, or with a good lie in the rough.

The No. 5 wood provides less distance and is used for poor lies. It is an extremely valuable club for players who cannot master the long irons.

Irons.   These clubs are of various lengths. Long irons (Nos. 2, 3, and 4) are designed to hit longer and lower shots.

The No. 5 iron is of medium length and is used as a beginning club primarily to learn the proper swing. It is an extremely efficient iron for the average shot out of the rough and for appropriate distances on par three holes.

The No. 6 iron is used for shorter distances and has more loft than the No. 5.

Nos. 7, 8, and 9 are short irons. The No. 7 is used for full-length approaches to the green, chip shots, and deep lies in the rough. Nos. 8 and 9 are used for pitch shots and for a variety of distances whenever extreme loft is required.

Club Selection.   A beginner's set of clubs should include the 3, 5, 7, and 9 irons, either the 1 and 3 or the 2 and 4 woods, and a putter. Because they produce greater loft, the 3 and 5 woods are superior to the 2 and 4, but they are not always included in the standard beginner's set of clubs.

Distance, loft, wind, and terrain are the major considerations in selecting the club for a given shot. The projected distance of a shot should be based on your average shot with a given club. In addition, you must consider the loft when negotiating any hazards. You must take into account the trajectory of the ball and whether it will clear the hazard before it begins to descend. The deeper the lie of the ball, the more loft is needed to get it out of the grass. Also remember that low shots should be hit into the wind and high shots with the wind at your back. Terrain must also be considered. For downhill shots, a lofted club should be used, and for uphill shots a less lofted club.

Other Clubs.   For sand and pitching, a wedge club can be used. This club is shorter and has more loft than the No. 9 iron. The sand wedge can be used *only* to get out of a sand trap. By regulation a player is allowed to carry only fourteen clubs, so that if he is using a full set he must choose between these two.

As for putters, there are two types from which to select. One is the weighted putter, preferred by most experienced players, and the other type, frequently used, is the blade. Work with both types to determine which is more comfortable and effective for you.

A final note: once you have evaluated the position of your ball and selected a club, proceed without hesitation. You must have confidence in your club so that you can concentrate on your swing!

Equipment

Golf equipment has come a long way from the days of the gutta-percha to today's liquid-center and tightly-wound ball and hickory shafts. These advances are in great degree responsible for a general improvement in the golfer's game. However, the beginning golfer should not expect his clubs to be programmed to break par the first time around, nor should he suffer delusion that the equipment which is most expensive or endorsed by name golfers will do that trick.

Buying Clubs. As a beginning golfer, consult your instructor before buying your first set of clubs. The instructor's advice is needed because the swing weights of different kinds of clubs differ. The grips should be of an all-weather material: *not* leather. You should buy either the 1 and 3 or 2 and 4 woods, the 3, 5, 7, and 9 irons, a putter, and a lightweight bag. This equipment should be of medium price. Medium-priced equipment is advisable because you will in all probability want a full set purchased *as a unit* once you become proficient. The original set can always be sold to another beginner at an appropriate time. Clubs *may* be added at random to a beginning set, but it is not advisable because of differences among clubs in balance, shaft, flex, and other factors.

Club Parts and Terms. Like any good sportsman, you should know the capabilities and limitations of your equipment. The various clubs have been described in the previous chapter. Now we will describe the characteristics of clubs in general.

Each club has four parts: the clubhead, the shaft, the grip, and the plug. (See figure 22.)

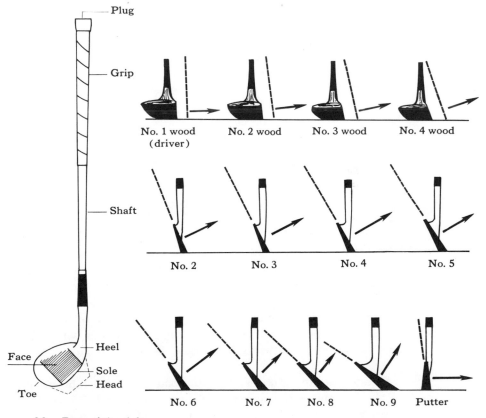

22   Parts of the club

The clubhead has four areas: the sole, the toe, the heel, and the face. The sole is the portion that is flat to the ground. The toe is the outermost point of the clubhead. The heel is the innermost point. The face is the striking surface.

The shaft is attached to the clubhead. Shafts are constructed of a wide variety of materials: aluminum, stainless steel, tempered steel, and fiberglass. The materials vary in price and flexibility. Golfers with less strength will probably want more flexible shafts, while stronger players will want stiffer shafts. As a general rule, price and personal choice are the only real criteria for selecting one type of shaft over another.

The grip is attached to the end of the shaft.

The plug is inserted in the end of the shaft.

The angle of the clubface is known as the loft of the club. The lower the number of the club, the less the loft. The length of the shaft decreases as the number of the club decreases. These factors naturally affect the shot. The low-numbered clubs produce longer and lower shots. With the higher numbers the loft and height of the ball increase as the distance decreases.

In wooden clubs, the heads become smaller as the number increases.

Care of Clubs, Bags, Shoes. Proper care of clubs and other equipment will not only extend their life but will result in more efficient performance.

Following each practice or game round, the clubs should be cleaned and dried with an absorbent cloth. Some protection against the elements can be achieved by rubbing the woods with a furniture paste wax. Leather grips should be treated with a leather conditioner.

In addition, the grooves of both wood and iron clubfaces must be cleaned out. A clogged face will prevent a good shot, and little spin can be obtained if the grooves are filled with dirt or mud. On the iron faces, a very fine steel wool, with mild detergent and water, should be used. A light coat of machine oil will prevent irons from rusting.

It is important to *avoid* prolonged storage of clubs and bags in the trunks of automobiles. The heat of a trunk steams damp clubs, resulting in rust. In addition, woods tend to swell and leather grips mildew.

The screws on woods should be tightened periodically and worn-out parts replaced.

Golf bags should always be placed in a dry area. Shoe trees are useful for damp shoes, although they can be stuffed with newspapers instead. With this kind of care, equipment should last for a number of years. When you decide to buy new equipment, your present equipment will be more valuable in sale or trade-in if you have cared for it properly.

Golf Carts.   Golf carts are not recommended for the beginner. There are two primary types of pull carts: bag carts (in which the bag is built into the cart) and folding carts. These can be rented. However, we recommend that the beginner carry his own clubs.

Clothing.   Appropriate clothing is as important to the golfer as proper equipment. You should wear clothing that is comfortable, permits a free turn of the torso during the swing, and allows free movement of the arms and legs.

Bermuda shorts, culottes, or a skirt that flairs are recommended for women. These also allow the instructor to view the knee position and movement during the learning period. Many golf courses will not allow women to play if they are dressed in slacks. Blouses, shirts, and jackets should be loose in the shoulder area, to allow for sufficient movement in the swing. In certain areas weatherproof jackets and wrap-around skirts may be advisable. For men, bermuda shorts or slacks and comfortable shirts are recommended.

Until you have made considerable progress, you should wear flat rather than spiked shoes. These should be the flat oxford type, with shoelaces to secure the foot and aid you in keeping your balance and anchoring your stance firmly throughout your swing. Tennis shoes are acceptable but loafers are not, because they tend to slip.

Putting

The essential differences in using the putter and using other clubs are in the grip and stance employed. There are many variations in putting style, but in order to avoid confusion and indecision, you should master the basic stroke before developing your own variation.

Grip. The beginning golfer should use the already mastered overlapping grip. However, the thumbs should be placed on *top* of the shaft, so that the elbows will spread slightly apart in a more relaxed position. This position also points the left elbow towards the cup, which is now the target. The more experienced player may use the reverse overlapping grip.

Stance. The feet and knees should be placed fairly close together in a manner that will afford good balance and some comfort. (See figures 23 and 24.) The feet should be parallel and perpendicular to the "inside track" of which we have spoken. Your weight should be on the insides of the feet, as earlier mentioned, and the knees should be moved toward one another (that is, the player should appear knock-kneed) so as to keep your weight from shifting.

23   Putting stance: clubface is square to line of putt

24   Putting stoke: clubface remains square as club is taken back

25
Putting stance,
front view

26
Putting stroke,
front view:
clubface is still
square after ball
is stroked
smoothly

Bend forward enough to place your head directly over the ball. To find the correct position, place the shaft between your eyes and over the ball.

The Stroke.   Draw an imaginary line between the clubface and the line of travel which the ball will follow to the cup. Then, on the average, the putter should be moved back about four inches and swung forward about *six* inches, to assure enough follow-through. (See figures 24, 25, and 26.) The lengths of the backswing and swing will differ with the strength of the player and the distance of the cup, but the same ratio between them should prevail.

From the beginning, concentrate on developing a fluid flow from the backswing through the follow-through. Do *not* jab at the ball. That will cause a backspin, so that the ball will stop before it arrives at the cup. On the contrary, an even, fluid stroke will provide overspin and give the ball an extra roll. Again, the length of the follow-through should be in direct proportion to length of the backswing.

Movement.   Up to this point, you have used your body for power in the swing. Now you are seeking accuracy and control. It is essential to recognize that the more parts of the body that are in movement, the greater the chance for the ball to move off the imaginary line that leads to the cup. Only the arms should move during the putt. While the arms should swing freely from the shoulders, the wrists must be kept firm and the hands should not turn. The head should also be kept still.

"Reading the Green."   Par on the green is two. It is therefore essential to place the first putt close enough to the cup so that the second shot will finish in the hole. Before the first putt you can help yourself by mentally drawing a circle about two feet in diameter around the cup. If you can then hit the first putt within that circle, the second should be comparatively easy.

Greens are not perfectly flat; therefore, they must be "read." When reading the green you will discover subtle hills and slopes virtually invisible at a distance. In putting you must compensate for these. For example, you may compensate for a slope by aiming from two to three inches—no more—toward the high side of the slope. In this situation one useful technique is to imagine a cup on the slope and use it as the terminal point of aim. If the degree of slope is in doubt, aim for the upper corner of the imaginary cup. Experience will increase your accuracy.

Greens are also "fast" or "slow." Generally, the shorter the grass the faster the green. The ball travels easier, farther, and with less effort on a fast green. Dry, hard surfaces, subtle contours, short grass, and downhill greens must also be compensated for. Only experience will teach you how to hit the ball in such circumstances.

Living Room Putting.
You can also practice putting in the living room (where "reading the carpet" is unnecessary. Here you can place a pair of rulers parallel to each other as the "track" and practice a smooth back-and-forth movement. A tin can may be used as the cup or target. As on the green, work for comfort, consistent accuracy, and confidence.

The Pitch Shot

The pitch shot is usually used when you are about 100 yards from the green. For this shot an 8 or 9 iron or a wedge club should be used to obtain loft so that the ball will land on the green near the cup and with minimum roll.

Experience will determine the appropriate club to use, but generally a long shot (from 90 to 110 yards) usually requires an 8 or 9 iron, while a medium shot (from 75 to 100 yards) requires a wedge club, depending on your strength.

Swing. In all cases the basic swing remains the same, though it varies in length according to the distance required. You must hit the ball in a way that will produce a backspin, so that the ball will not roll past the flag or off the green. (See figures 27 through 31.) This is achieved by hitting the ball with a firm stroke while maintaining a steady head position. In addition, be sure not to raise your body, waist, arms, or head during the stroke; if you do you will "top" the ball, producing no loft and causing the ball to roll beyond the cup.

Hit the ball with a descending blow but do not chop, dig, or lunge at the ball. If you hit properly, the blade will dig a slight divot, resulting in a highly lofted shot that will drop on the green with very little roll. You should, of course, aim for the pin so that you can then putt the hole in one shot.

27
Pitch shot,
address position

28   Pitch shot, top of backswing: note that back is toward target

29   Pitch shot, downswing: knees are driving toward target

30
Pitch shot: ball
is hit first, and
then turf on
follow-through

31
Pitch shot: on
follow-through,
clubhead is still
on line to target

Sand Traps

Getting out of a sand trap requires an "explosion" shot with either a 9 iron, a pitching wedge, or, preferably, a sand wedge. The club-head should hit the sand about an inch behind the ball, thus providing a cushion of sand that will prevent the ball from traveling too far.

Stance. A firm stance is necessary and can be obtained by wiggling the feet to obtain a solid footing. The point at which the club hits the sand should be lined up with the center of the stance. You should concentrate on that spot rather than the back of the ball. Golf rules prevent grounding the club in a hazard, since doing so could elevate the ball and improve the lie.

Swing. The same swing should be used as in hitting a pitch shot. During the shot concentrate especially on your follow-through so that the sand will not stop or delay the smooth-flowing arc of the clubhead. It is helpful to imagine that you are pitching the *sand* rather than the ball to the green. If too much sand is taken, the ball will remain in the trap. If too little is taken, the ball will travel too far over the green.

After the shot, as a matter of golf etiquette, rake the sand smooth where you have made depressions by walking, standing, or hitting the ball.

The "Chip and Run" Shot

Although this shot is also known as the "pitch and run" shot, we prefer to call it the "chip and run" to distinguish it clearly from the pitch shot.

Purpose. This shot is one of the most valuable of all golf shots for both the beginner and expert player. It should be used when you are about 35 yards from the green, with no intervening obstructions such as sand traps, bushes, or elevations. Whenever possible it should be selected over the pitch shot because it results in a good loft with a bouncy roll. In addition, it is safer than a pitch shot from the same distance because, unlike the pitch, if the ball is not properly hit but topped, it will not overshoot the green.

Technique. For the chip and run shot, use a 5, 6, or 7 iron, depending on the required loft. The ball should travel in the air one-third of the distance to the cup and on the ground for two-thirds of the distance. Consequently, the first bounce should be on the green.

In preparing for the shot, use the "human robot" exercise mentioned earlier. The ball should be located in the middle of the stance. The club should be held half-way down the grip. (See figures 32 through 34.) The feet should be close together, there

32
Chip and run
shot, address
position

33   Chip and run shot: striking the ball

34   Chip and run shot: striking the ball, side view

should be no weight shift during the shot, and the hands should be in position ahead of the club, as shown in figure 33. The wrists must be stable, and the arms should swing straight back and straight through. In general, the swing technique is the same as that for putting, except that the elbows should be kept closer together.

If these procedures are followed, the ball will develop an over-spin and get a good roll to the cup. The primary danger in this shot is in hitting the ground before the ball. This can be prevented by keeping the hands ahead of the club, as mentioned above.

Strategy of Playing the Course

Need for Practice. It is essential for you as a beginning golfer to work through all the preliminary steps of learning the game before playing your first round. These steps include a thorough understanding of the instruction, continual practice of the exercises and individual shots, and knowledge of the capabilities of each club, the rules of the game, and golf etiquette.

Each of these elements must be studied and practiced to the point that you are both proficient and comfortable before playing your first round. The reason is basic: a mastery of fundamentals produces confidence, and confidence helps produce the best in any competitor. Aside from the matter of attitude, a mastery of fundamentals means that you can conserve your energies for planning and carrying out your strategy, and need not be hampered by worries about the mechanics of the game. What sort of performance would a pianist give if he had to look at every single key before striking it?

Elements of Strategy. As a general practice, play each hole with a plan in mind: make a mental note of where you expect to place each shot on the fairway. You should decide your strategy before teeing up for the first hole. Considerations include the distance of the hole, the placement of the flag, the trouble spots (trees, roughs, sand traps), and your best shots. If the flag or trouble spots cannot be seen, inquire about them from someone who has played the course.

In deciding strategy it is especially important for you to know your best shots. Self-analysis and honest appraisal are basic. If you are not realistic, strategy has no real meaning. For example, let us take the case of a par 5, 455-yard hole. If your best shot is 150 yards, arithmetic will tell you that you cannot possibly hit the green in the regulation three shots. Therefore, do not try to knock the cover off the ball, but employ your natural swing and play for position. This means that you should concentrate on a good swing that will take the ball down the fairway, out of trouble, and in a good position. The third shot should place you in a position from which a short-approach chip shot will place your ball on the green where you can one-putt the cup.

Even an experienced golfer can all too often think in terms of the *distance to the hole* rather than the *steps which will lead him to the cup.* With such an attitude he attempts to force each stroke for distance in order to reach the green faster than is mathematically possible. As a result a golfer can lose control and must sacrifice strokes to get out of unconsidered trouble spots. Planning in terms of his best shots and the trouble spots of the course will put the golfer ahead of the game.

Hitting Par.   A word more about strategy and the beginning golfer. Strategy is not reality, and beginning golfers must remember that only continued practice and experience will allow them to employ strategy to the best advantage. Rarely will a beginning golfer par a hole. However, you should establish your own *par,* according to your capabilities and limitations. With further practice and experience in developing a "longer ball," you should eventually be able to hit par.

Now that basic general elements of strategy have been established, consideration must be given to individual shots and the trouble spots that may be encountered.

Determining Distance.   After the tee shot, you must determine the remaining distance to be covered, which club to use, and how far to hit the ball. The distance, of course, can be computed by subtracting the length of the tee shot from the total distance to the hole. You should then determine which club to use on the basis of the distance you have consistently hit in practice with each club.

With experience, distance can be determined accurately by sight. Beginners should be aware of certain common distortions. A narrow fairway, for example, appears to be longer than a wide one.

Obstructions.   Depressions in the terrain and climatic conditions must also be taken into consideration, as well as the lie of the ball. If the lie is bad, you should consider several new factors. For example, if the ball is in the rough, it must be remembered that the deeper the rough, the more loft is necessary. You should try to get out of the rough and back to the fairway by the most direct route. As a beginner you may have special problems. In general you should sacrifice distance for position. You should also become aware of hazards in the immediate area. If you hit too long a ball or hit it inaccurately, you may find yourself in another trouble spot.

Hitting the ball from a fairway trap also presents special problems. Loft is needed, but because of the distance remaining, the loft should not be as great as when hitting out of a trap near the green. The average fairway trap requires a No. 5 iron, but it must be remembered that some traps are deeper than others, so that you must consider which club is most appropriate. A fairway trap shot should be hit clean; that is, the club should *not* disturb the sand.

Hitting the sand with the club naturally tends to kill the distance of the shot.

Hitting the ball from behind a tree provides special problems. You must consider the lie of the ball in relation to its distance behind the tree, in order to decide whether the ball can be hit under the branches of the tree without striking them or whether enough loft can be provided to top the tree. In addition, the distances probable with each method should be considered. If the foliage is so thick and high that neither choice is possible, you must employ your best alternate shot to assure a good lie on the fairway. The decision must be based not only on the physical conditions in which you find your ball but also on an honest appraisal of your own abilities.

Hillside Shots.   Probably the most difficult shots in golf occur when the ball lies on a hillside and you must make physical adjustments to maintain your balance, coordination, steady foot placement, and a body position permitting a swing that provides the desired distance and position.

When the ball is on a downhill slope, place your right foot *opposite* the ball rather than centering the ball between your feet as mentioned earlier. The more severe the slope, the closer the ball should be to a perpendicular line extending from the right heel. To determine the ball placement in relation to the feet, take a practice swing. The bottom of the swing is the point at which the club will hit the ground. Note your position and move forward so that the club will hit the ball at that same spot.

If, as is usual, you are standing with your right foot higher on the slope than your left foot, you must *not* compensate by leaning to your left. You should use an open stance, with the left foot slightly to the rear of the "track" mentioned in earlier chapters. Since the slope of the hill will also tend to pull your weight forward, you should place your weight on your heels to prevent gravity from destroying your balance.

In addition, the awkward position during a downhill shot may encourage you to hit the ball harder than usual. However, this will result only in loss of balance and a bad shot. To compound the problem, the ball will almost always tend to travel to the right. To compensate for this, you should aim slightly to the left.

In addition to compensating for the special problems offered by the downhill slope, you should know how to use the slope advantageously. For example, you can use the loft of the clubface to best advantage by following the contours of the hill in your follow-through. You should also pick your club carefully. If the same shot were to be made on a flat surface with a 3 iron for maximum distance, you should probably use a 4 iron on the hillside shot because of the loft that the hill will take away from the shot.

In a sidehill shot, in which the ball is positioned higher than your feet, you should use a normal club for the distance desired. However, you should shorten the club length by "choking" it. You should place your left heel opposite the ball; although you will therefore swing more horizontally, your swing will have a more normal feel than most hillside shots.

For uphill shots you must, of course, use a strategy opposite to what you use for downhill shots. Your left leg will be higher than your right, so that you are again confronted with the problem of balance. Your instinct will tell you to pivot against gravity and transfer your weight to your left leg. However, you should use the contour of the hill by placing your left heel opposite the ball. The greater the slope the closer the ball should be to a perpendicular line extending from the heel. Since the hill can provide extra loft, a less lofted club should be used.

Simplified Golf Rules

The rules of tournament golf are complex, and are agreed upon and modified by the Royal and Ancient Golf Club of St. Andrews in Scotland and the United States Golf Association. A simplified list of rules is published by the National Golf Foundation, 804 Merchandise Mart, Chicago, Illinois, 60654. The following is a general description of common situations.

A full round of golf consists of eighteen holes. Beginners, however, may play only nine holes. As a general rule, you must not touch the ball from tee-off until the last putt drops into the cup. If the ball must be touched, there are rules covering where it must be moved and how. Every stroke or attempt made during the game must be counted.

The teeing ground is defined by two tee markers. You may tee off anywhere within two club lengths behind these markers. If the ball falls off the tee, it may be replaced without counting that as a stroke. However, if you swing and miss, you must count that as a stroke.

Certain plays and situations require a penalty against the player. If for example, you lose the ball or hit it out of bounds, you incur a penalty of "loss of distance plus one stroke": in other words, you must play the next stroke from a spot as close as possible to that from which the original play was made, and you must add one penalty stroke to your score.

If you hit a water hazard, you get a penalty of one stroke. You then drop the ball behind the hazard, on a straight line extending from the hole through the place where the ball hit the hazard. You *may* play the ball from the hazard without penalty, but you may *not* ground your club before taking the shot. In the case of a lateral hazard (one which lies parallel to the line of play), you may drop the ball within two club lengths of the edge of the hazard, opposite the point where the ball entered the hazard, but no nearer the hole.

You may hit an "unplayable" lie. You are the sole judge of when the ball is unplayable. In that case you have three options. First you may play the next stroke from a spot as close as possible to the place from which the original ball was hit, with a penalty of loss of distance plus one stroke, as described above. Second, you may play the ball from a spot within an area of two club lengths but no nearer the hole, without penalty. Third, you may play the ball from a spot behind the unplayable lie, on a straight line extending from the hole through the place where the ball finally landed, under penalty of one stroke.

In some instances you may touch the ball *without* penalty. If the ball lies in casual water, ground under repair, a hole, or a cast or runway made by a bird or animal, you may lift the ball and drop it as near as possible (but not nearer the hole) on ground which lacks these conditions.

If the ball lies next to an obstacle or artificial obstruction, such as a drinking fountain, ball washer, bench, or storage shed (as long as it is not marked out of bounds), you may drop the ball within two club lengths of the obstruction but no nearer the hole.

To save time, if a ball is thought to be lost or out of bounds, you may play with a new ball until you reach the place where the original ball may be. If it is then discovered to be lost or out of bounds, the penalty is imposed. If not, the player continues with the original ball, without penalty.

Sometimes another's ball will interfere with the line of a player's putt. In medal play, the player may then either mark the ball or putt it. In match play he asks his opponent to mark it. As a general rule, the player may clean his ball on the green but he may not change balls unless his ball is damaged.

In general, the best way for the beginner to learn the rules is to ask his instructor about them when he comes across a situation he does not understand. Other golfers may confuse the beginner by offering contradictory or simplified advice. The score the golfer records should reflect his game according to the official rules; otherwise it will give a false picture of how well he is doing.

Etiquette

A wise man, doubtless the product of a diplomatic corps, once said that the essence of etiquette is being able to eat a piece of celery between two crackers without making a sound. Although golf etiquette is not yet that exacting, there are rules of behavior, both written and unwritten, that will enhance enjoyment of the game both for you and your partners and for the other golfers, too.

Basic advice, of course, is to use common sense in conducting yourself on the course, and, paraphrasing the Golden Rule, to conduct yourself as you wish others to do.

The general rules of golf etiquette are universally agreed upon. There should be no talking, moving, or dropping of clubs when another player is setting up and making his shot. Golfers should help each other spot balls. They should also keep a steady pace and be ready to take their shots as soon as possible.

Steady Pace. It is easy for you to determine if you are keeping a steady pace. You take your turn when you have determined that the players ahead of you are beyond your longest shot. If no one is playing the hole ahead, you are not maintaining the normal speed of play. At the same time it is important the players behind are not held up in their play. If they are kept waiting by your normal style of play, or if there is a delay in searching for a ball, they should be allowed to play through. The USGA allows five minutes for finding a ball, but three minutes should be sufficient in a social game.

The most flagrant violation of etiquette is to fail to take your shot in turn. The player who is farthest from the hole has the first shot, so the other players should have ample time to line up their shots and proceed quickly. This does *not* mean, of course, that you should hurry your shot by rushing your golf swing. As we mentioned earlier, you should take one practice swing, waggle a bit for relaxation, and then swing in the manner in which you have been taught. The real pace in playing is achieved by walking fast to the point of lie.

Etiquette on the Green.

Observance of the rules of etiquette is crucial on or near the green. This is a time of extreme concentration for all players, and certain rules are obligatory:

1. Replace divots. This is common courtesy anywhere on the course, but it is particularly important on the green. Holes made in the turf by dragging spikes across the green should also be covered.

2. Rake all marks made in a trap, whether they are footprints or the result of club swings.

3. Repair ball marks on the green.

4. Keep from getting in the line of vision of those taking shots.

5. Do not pull or ride a cart on the green. The grass is short there, and the tire marks create permanent damage to the green.

6. Place your golf bag on one side of the green, preferably in the direction of the next tee.

7. If your ball is in line with a fellow player's putt, use a ball marker or coin.

8. The person closest to the pin attends to the flag. He should

ask the putter whether he wishes the flag stuck in or out of the cup.

9. Never walk across the line which a player's ball is to travel. This may disturb his concentration, and the footprints will create unexpected contours on the green.

10. After you have "holed out," remove the ball from the cup. A ball left in the cup could create a bounce for the next ball entering it.

11. The first person to hole out should replace the flag after the last player completes his final shot. This is both common courtesy and a time saver.

12. Mark your score *after* leaving the green, so that your group can move on and allow shot range for the players following. The player should, of course, keep his score honestly and accurately. If he does not, he will never really know just how much he is improving. In addition, cheating will become obvious to the other members of the group and the golfer may find it hard to find company in subsequent play.

Attitudes.   Like most games, the game of golf is one of self-control. Rage does not improve it. Unfortunately, tempers do occasionally flare, usually because the golfer is frustrated by his own performance. It is fairly axiomatic that sore losers are bad players. Moreover, foul language is offensive to others, and the throwing of clubs not only reflects upon a player's maturity but is also extremely dangerous to other golfers.

The player should not bother to brood over bad shots. Reviewing the last hole will not correct mistakes, and the golfer should be concentrating on his next shot as he approaches his lie.

Following a round, it is *not* proper protocol to ask others their scores. An appropriate question is "How did you do?" This leaves the other golfer the choice of offering his score or answering with a generality. Winners should be congratulated and losers offered condolences.

Etiquette of Play.   The basic rules of golf should be well known to every golfer. The USGA publishes a pamphlet on rules which may be obtained at golf and sports shops. Illustrated rule books are also available.

It is usual for players to use the same ball throughout each hole. If the ball is cut or damaged, it is permissible to replace it.

On a par three hole, when every member of the playing party is on the green, it is common courtesy to motion oncoming players to hit up.

The golfer should always keep his golf bag with him. Left lying, it will be in the way of other golfers and may hold up their game. No golfer should share his bag with another player. It is inconvenient, and most courses will not admit players without individual bags and clubs. Before beginning a round, each golfer should be certain that he has sufficient balls, tees, and other necessary equipment. Golfers should dress for comfort, as discussed above, but also according to the customs and regulations of the course being played.

Observance of golf etiquette will aid you not only in your playing but in your relationships with others. Failure to observe it will inhibit your game and may ostracize you from many people who play golf for fun and pleasure.

Playing for Fun

Although you should approach the game with the idea that it is designed for relaxation and recreation, the element of competition, of one sort or another, is always present in the game. Probably the most exacting competition is with one's self: the golfer is in effect always playing against himself and his best previous performance. However, there are various types of competition among players that can be introduced to lend variety to the game.

TYPES OF TOURNAMENTS.

Medal Play. This is the simplest kind of tournament, in which the total score determines the winner.

Match. This game consists of hole-by-hole competition. The individual winning the most holes for the round wins the match. When the term "three up" is used, that means a player has won three more holes than his opponent. When a player is ahead by more holes than remain in the game, the match can be considered concluded, although it can be continued if so desired. It should be noted that this is the only game in which a player can concede a putt. Conceding a putt is usually considered a matter of courtesy, since it speeds the play.

Two-Ball.   The two-ball game is played by two sets of partners. The partners hit alternate shots with the same ball. After the drive from the tee, the partners may choose which of them will hit the second shot. This is the *only* occasion on which they make a choice. The decision should be made on the basis of the abilities of the players and the placement and distance of the upcoming shot. From then until the end of the hole the partners must make alternate shots. The winning team is determined on the basis of the lowest total score.

Pinehurst.   This game was named for a golf course. The game is begun as each partner tees off. They then trade balls for the second shot. Following this shot, the partners must determine which one ball the two of them will finish the hole with. If partner A has hit the second shot, the partner B must hit the third shot: they alternate in this way throughout the hole. For players of differing ability, this game is an excellent equalizer, as in mother-daughter, father-son, and couples' tournaments.

Best Ball Tournament.   Each player of a twosome plays his own ball. A record of the score of the best ball on each hole is kept through the eighteenth hole. The partners with the lowest combined score of best balls are the winners.

Bingle, Bangle, or Bungle.   Whichever of these names is used, it is the same game. Players compete as individuals. One point each is given a player for being first on the green, nearest the hole, and first in the cup: a total of three points per hole. The player with the highest total number of points wins.

Low Putt.   As the name implies, the player with fewest putts wins the game. This game is an equalizer, and gives the new golfer with a good putting game a chance over the experienced player.

Conclusion

You now have taken the first series in an endless number of lessons in golf. We say "endless" because no one ever will beat the game once and for all. The top professionals will not beat it; you will not beat it. But therein lies the fascination of the game. There always is room for improvement, and your stiffest competition will be yourself and the best round you have ever played.

Golf is a difficult sport, and mastery does not come easily. Its physical disciplines are not related to those of any other sport, so that you cannot rely upon transferring techniques or muscle memories. Because golf is an individual sport, you cannot rely on the rest of the team if you play poorly. Unlike a tennis player, who reacts to the shots given to him, you cannot even "rely" upon your opponent.

Additionally, your success at golf does not necessarily depend upon your physical strength or build. Mental and physical discipline must be developed so that you can coordinate mind and body to execute your game. When these elements are developed so that you experience the joy of a smooth swing or an exacting putt, golf becomes not only a pleasure but a constructive emotional outlet.

These accomplishments can be shared with persons of mixed

ability: members of a family or friends. Experienced golfers agree that the golf course is one of the best places for getting to know another person, his character, his personality, his emotions.

No longer is golf a game only for the affluent. Because of the proliferation of municipal courses, it no longer is necessary to belong to a country club to be a part of the game. And it costs no more than a movie.

Along with the emotions and accomplishments go the responsibilities. Those who love the game and seek to perpetuate it must exert their influence to keep land taxes within reason and prevent fairways from becoming freeways or bases for industrial complexes. Although the number of golfers and spectators of golf has risen appreciably in recent years, golf courses have not been created in proportion to that growth. And so golf has become more than just a private game for the affluent in Yonkers. It is national, and it is individual: national in its scope and individual in its challenge and appeal to people.

Glossary

Address   The position the player takes with feet, body, and club behind the ball before taking his stroke.

Apron   Edge of the putting green.

Away   The ball farthest from the hole.

Back nine, in nine   Last nine holes on an eighteen-hole course.

Bunker   A depression or mound of sand. A grass-covered area within a bunker or bordering it is not part of the hazard.

Casual water   Water that accumulates accidentally on the golf course and is not intended to be there.

Chip and run shot   A low shot of thirty-five yards or less which rolls towards the target.

Divot   Grass that is removed by a golfer's swing.

Fairway   Area of closely cropped grass between the tee and the green.

Front nine, out nine   First nine holes on an eighteen-hole course.

Greenies   Balls that come from the tee to rest on the green.

Grounding the club   Resting the sole of the club on the ground.

Hazard   There are two types. Sand traps or bunkers are mounds or depressions of sand. Water hazards (lakes, rivers, etc.) are usually defined by stakes or lime lines.

Hole   The hole is $4\frac{1}{4}$ inches in diameter and at least 4 inches deep. If a lining is used, it must be sunk at least 1 inch below the putting green surface.

Hole out   To drop the ball in the cup.

Honor   The honor of teeing off first is given to the person who had the lowest score on the previous hole. On the fairway or green, the honor is given to the person whose ball lies farthest from the pin.

Hook   Flight of a golf ball which begins straight but then arcs to the left (for right-handed player).

Lie   Situation of the ball on the course.

Out of bounds   Area off the golf course. It is usually marked off by fences.

Pitch shot   A highly lofted shot used to overcome obstacles in approaching the green. It lands with little or no roll.

Preferred lie   The name of a local rule which permits the player to improve his lie on the fairway. This varies with the course condition and local custom. Sometimes known as "winter rules."

Pull   Flight of a golf ball which goes directly to the left without any deviation (for right-handed player).

Push   Flight of a golf ball which goes directly to the right without any deviation (for right-handed player).

Putting green   Area which contains the cup. The grass is extremely short and smooth.

Rough   Area of longer grass or weeds on either side of the fairway.

Skied   A ball is skied when it travels straight up into the air with a minimum of forward movement.

Slice   Flight of a golf ball which begins straight but then arcs to the right (for right-handed player).

Teeing ground   Elevated ground for teeing off. Tees for men, women, and championship play are denoted by color and placed at various designated distances.

Thin   A shot is thin when the ball is struck slightly above center and achieves very little height. It does not travel quite as low as the topped ball.

Top   To hit the ball above center, causing a low rolling shot.

Whiff   To miss the ball entirely on a stroke.

Selected Readings

Armour, Tommy. *How to Play Your Best Golf All the Time* (New York: Simon & Schuster, 1953)

Aultman, Dick. *The Square-To-Square Golf Swing* (New York: Simon & Schuster, 1970)

Bruce, Ben and Davies, Evelyn. *Beginning Golf* (Belmont, Calif.: Wadsworth, 1968)

Charles, Bob. *Lefthanded Golf* (Englewood Cliffs, N.J.: Prentice-Hall, 1965)

Cochran, Alastair and Stobbs, John. *The Search for the Perfect Swing* (Philadelphia: Lippincott, 1968)

Fossum, Bruce G. and Dagraedt, Mary. *Golf* (Boston: Allyn & Bacon, 1969)

Jacobs, John and Bowden, Ken. *Practical Golf* (New York: Quadrangle, 1972)

Moran, Sharron. *Golf Is a Woman's Game* (New York: Hawthorn, 1971)

Nance, Virginia L. and Davis, Elwood C. *Golf* (Dubuque, Iowa: W. C. Brown, 1971)

Nicklaus, Jack and Wind, Herbert W. *The Greatest Game of All* (New York: Simon & Schuster, 1969)

Toski, Bob. *The Touch System for Better Golf* (New York: Simon & Schuster, 1971)

Useful Addresses

National Golf Foundation, Inc.
The Merchandise Mart
Chicago, IL 60654

U.S.G.A. (United States Golf Association)
40 West 38th Street
New York, NY 10016